CANARY BREEDING
KW-131

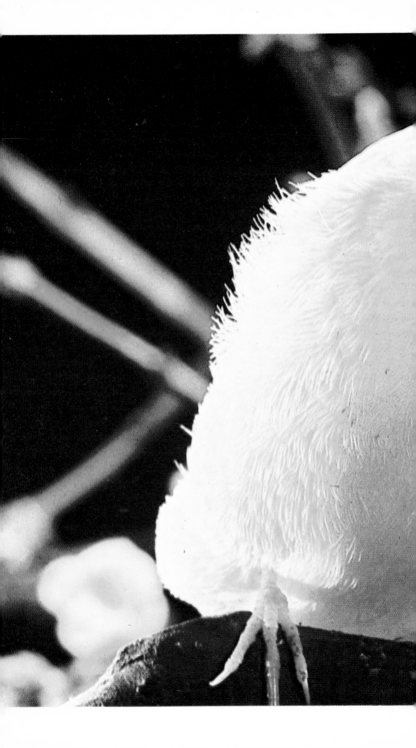

CONTENTS

Photo Credits:
Harry V. Lacey; p. 5-8, 15, 16 (#1 & 2), 20 (bottom), 28, 32, 33, 48, 50, 52, 53, 78 (#1 & 4), 83 (#1 & 3), 86 (#4), 91 (#1, 2 & 4). Horst Mueller (Vogelpark Walsrode); p. 10, 11, 14, 18, 19, 22, 23, 26, 27, 30, 31, 66, 67, 75, 78 (2 & 3), 83 (#2), 86 (#1, 2, 3 & 5). Walter Preschel; p. 16 (#3), 20 (left). Dr. Matthew M. Vriends; p. 70, 71, 91 (#3).

Pages 2 & 3:
Who would have ever guessed that this beautiful bird is a descendant of a dull green bird, the original canary from the Canary Islands!

Pages 94 & 95:
Gloster Fancy Canaries. Photo by Harry V. Lacey.

Originally published in German by Franckh'sche Verlagshandlung, W. Keller & Co., Stuttgart 1969 under the title *Kanarienrassen.*First edition © 1969 by Franckh'sche Verlagshandlung.

© 1979, © 1989 by T.F.H. Publications, Inc. Ltd. for English translation. A considerable amount of additional new material has been added to the literal German-English translation, including but not limited to additional photographs. Copyright is also claimed for this new material.

TRANSLATED BY CHRISTA AHRENS

Distributed in the UNITED STATES by T.F.H. Publications, Inc., One T.F.H. Plaza, Neptune City, NJ 07753; in CANADA to the Pet Trade by H & L Pet Supplies Inc., 27 Kingston Crescent, Kitchener, Ontario N2B 2T6; Rolf C. Hagen Ltd., 3225 Sartelon Street, Montreal 382 Quebec; in CANADA to the Book Trade by Macmillan of Canada (A Division of Canada Publishing Corporation), 164 Commander Boulevard, Agincourt, Ontario M1S 3C7; in ENGLAND by T.F.H. Publications Limited, Cliveden House/Priors Way/Bray, Maidenhead, Berkshire SL6 2HP, England; in AUSTRALIA AND THE SOUTH PACIFIC by T.F.H. (Australia) Pty. Ltd., Box 149, Brookvale 2100 N.S.W., Australia; in NEW ZEALAND by Ross Haines & Son, Ltd., 18 Monmouth Street, Grey Lynn, Auckland 2, New Zealand; in the PHILIPPINES by Bio-Research, 5 Lippay Street, San Lorenzo Village, Makati Rizal; in SOUTH AFRICA by Multipet Pty. Ltd., 30 Turners Avenue, Durban 4001. Published by T.F.H. Publications, Inc. Manufactured in the United States of America by T.F.H. Publications, Inc.

CANARY
BREEDING

KLAUS SPEICHER

New color canary. This mutation occurred in England and New Zealand in 1908. The recessive white of today, as pictured, is a descendant of the New Zealand mutation.

Silver Brown Opal. This is the opal mutation in a brown canary of the recessive white series. Both "brown" and "opal" refer to mutations involving the melanin pigments.

Feather structure (buff). Canaries' feather structure is one of the factors that gives most varieties their pleasing sleek appearance.

Introduction

What to do with one's spare time has become a much-discussed problem of the day. The word "hobby" is in the vogue. Hobbies have mobilized whole branches of industry to help us in our pursuit of diversification of our free-time activities.

Interestingly, with the growing increase in leisure time there has also come a rise in membership figures of the so-often-scorned breeding societies of small indoor animals. Nowadays it is no longer possible for everyone to keep small animals; the average home tends to be unsuitable for

Yorkshire Canary. This bird was created during the last quarter of the nineteenth century from crossings involving the common canary, the Lancashire Plainhead, the Norwich (old fashioned type) and the Belgian.

Gold Agate Melanin Pastel, Intensive. In Holland, in the early 1900's, a pale ash-gray hen was bred from an ordinary green x green mating. The variety was given the name "agate." The "gold" here indicates the yellow ground.

the purpose. And yet the number of hobbyist breeders specializing in "indoor animals" continues to rise. The term "hobbyist breeders," in the widest sense, embraces all animal lovers who breed animals in their own homes. Aquarium fishes, birds and small mammals have taken the place of those domestic animals that were not only useful to man but also valued as "companions." There have, of course, always been animals by man's side. The hunting nomad in days of yore, the peasant who had become adapted to a settled life, the Eskimo in his dog-sled, the mounted warrior—all had (and still have) animals as companions and friends and lived with them in mutual dependence. Today the "indoor animals" are increasingly replacing the domestic animals of the past, and it is thanks to these small creatures that we remain in contact with innocent, unspoilt Nature.

An incomparably more fascinating hobby than that of just keeping pets is to breed animals. Every serious breeder has to be familiar with Nature's laws of heredity if he wants to be really successful. What is required of him, in other words, is a degree of genuine scientific interest in the study of animal-breeding.

Equally important, however, for those who want to produce pure breeds, is that they never lose sight of the image of the ideal breeding result with all its superior qualities—and that they always should make a critical comparison between their actual achievements and this ideal. The breeder has to be not only a scientist but an artist as well. He has to take an active part in the shaping of Nature. The laws applied are always the same, whether the animals to be cultivated are Thoroughbred race-horses or Gloucester canaries. What makes a first-rate breeder is a detailed knowledge of the whys and wherefores of the genetic transmission of certain characteristics. Canaries are particularly favored as breeding objects. They do not take up much space, and the fact that a new generation can be produced each year offers the breeder an opportunity to visibly influence the developmental history of some breed or variation of his choice.

It does not much matter, by the way, how many pairs a breeder employs for his experiments. A breeder with four pairs can be more successful than one who uses twenty but does not know the hereditary material of his animals and, therefore, "mismatches" the pairs.

The exhibiting of animals has become an increasingly popular sport with competitive-minded hobbyist breeders over the last decade or so, particularly with regard to canaries. In the early days, German breeding-clubs devoted their interest exclusively to songsters of the Harz Mountain Roller variety. Today bird fanciers can follow their personal preferences and choose birds from anywhere in the world and from among a seemingly endless range of colors, types, head-dresses and shapes. However, it should not be "taste" alone that decides for or against a particular variety. The crucial factors are accommodation, care and the time one will be able to devote to the birds. Singing varieties, for example, require about two months of uninterrupted "training"; that is, they require a period of "tutoring" in solitary confinement. During this time the breeder must devote a few hours to his feathered pupils every day if he wants to succeed. Furthermore, the prospective singing birds must be kept at room temperature.

Where birds bred primarily for color are concerned it is of prime importance during the molting season to provide a varied diet rich in carotene, which is essential if the red coloring is to intensify.

For breeding "shapes" we need bigger cages, and for certain varieties of shapes separate show and training cages have to be set up. In addition—once again—time, patience and sympathetic understanding are necessary.

All this should be taken into careful consideration by the prospective breeder before he decides on his purchase.

Gloster Fancy consort. The head must be broad and round at every point, with good rise of the center of the skull. The eyebrows must be heavy and showing brow.

14

Border Fancy Canary. This is a self blue. As you can see, the blue is really more of a slate gray with a mixture of brown.

15

1

2

3

However, having decided which "line" is best suited to him, the breeder will derive a great deal of pleasure from his hobby, and experience is of course the best teacher anyway!

Novices tend to be confused by the multitude of color shades and varieties in which the canary exists. This little book is intended to serve as a guide through the maze. A book of this limited scope can offer no more than a survey and introduction, but I hope it will stimulate hobbyists into studying the subject of canary breeding in greater depth.

Klaus Speicher

. Gloster Canary. In any crested variety there exist two types, the crested bird itself and its plain-headed counterpart; each of which is an intrinsic part of the breed as a whole. 2. Border Canary. The Border Canary is known for its alertness. Careful selection of well-colored stock is essential. 3. Young healthy looking canaries are a goal for any serious aviculturist.

Gold Yellow, Intensive. The all-yellow variety is the best known kind of canary.

18

Red Agate Lipochrome-pastel, Intensive. Note the eye and malar lines characteristic of agate birds.

Selection is the road to success. *Left:* Buff Norwich cock and yellow Norwich hen. *Below:* A border Fancy self-blue.

Selecting Birds for Breeding

Usually there is already a single canary (almost always a male) in the house by the time the decision is made to try and breed canaries. So only a hen, a partner for the cock bird already in residence, needs to be bought. Breeding stock is best purchased in the fall, when the molt is over and the birds look smart in their new plumage. At this time of the year the breeders stock both young birds and older ones in a much larger number than at any other time. In other words, they will be only too pleased to get rid of some. Another reason why prices are favorable in the fall is that the birds will have to be fed right through the winter months up to the time when they mate in the spring.

The silver brown phaeo-ino is one of the latest mutations established.

Red Isabel, Nonintensive. The presence of the isabel factor is most apparent on the mantle.

So as right from the start to give his canary-breeding attempts every chance to succeed, the novice should make sure that the breeding pairs are properly matched. First of all he needs to know which variety the cock bird already in his possession belongs to. Is it a song canary or a color canary? It is always regrettable when, out of sheer carelessness, these varieties are crossed and years of effort put in by the breeders come to nothing as a result. Since the canaries start to breed at about the beginning of spring, we practically have the whole winter to look for a suitable hen. The breeder should, however, have his pairs complete at least six weeks before the mating season starts. This is to give the birds a chance to become acclimatized.

Which birds we choose is, above anything else, a matter of personal preference. We must like them, because they are to give us pleasure. It is quite immaterial which variety we select. There are no "commonplace" and "better" varieties as such; fashion trends are what makes the price of certain varieties and color shades shoot up from time to time. The relatively expensive birds tend to be new mutations whose prices will go down when they have ceased to be rare "novelties." It is the competition to obtain rarities as well as their supply that controls prices, as collectors in other fields of interest can confirm. What matters above all is that the canaries we have purchased be healthy and able to breed.

Most people favor young birds. A smooth plumage, clear, alert eyes and a lively disposition indicate that the bird is in good health. Experienced breeders, however, prefer their breeding birds to differ in age. They want to pair a young cock with a hen over a year old, or an older cock with a young hen so that the breeding experience of the older partner can help matters to proceed smoothly. There can be no doubt that it is an advantage to have a bird that has already proved itself to be a good parent. Whether the canaries remain capable of breeding until quite late in life depends on how much is demanded of them in the business of breeding each year. Generally speaking, two clutches per year can be considered normal. If we do not expect more than that of our birds, we should be able to breed successfully with one pair for six to seven years. If, on the other hand, a cock bird is used to serve several hens every year he will be worn out much sooner. Similarly, a breeder who expects three, four or even five clutches from his hens in one season—and perhaps in addition leaves the rearing of the young solely to them—is sure to exhaust his birds much more quickly.

For a closer examination of a breeding bird's state of health we hold it firmly in the hand and blow into the feathers of the abdomen. To check the physical condition of potential breeders before buying them is an established custom among canary breeders. It also makes it easier to tell the sexes apart.

Healthy cock birds ready for mating show a "spike," in the form of a projection of skin around the cloaca. The belly is slightly sunken and of a normal flesh color. If the intestines are swollen and clealy visible beneath the skin (perhaps red and inflamed), the bird is sick. The sternum must be properly enclosed by muscles, and the whole breast should feel well filled out. A sharply protruding sternum is a sign of severe emaciation. Any bird found to suffer from this is very ill indeed.

The hen has a slightly more elongated body. The cloacal region is not as prominent as in the cock bird. If a small "spike" is present, it points rather more towards the tail. If we remind ourselves of the physiological function this part has during the act of mating, we cannot go far wrong when looking here for help with sexual differentiation.

The breeder wishing to start off with several hens would do well to keep one or more hens as "spares." Disturbances do occur and might cause a hen to "drop out"—in which case having a spare hen would be a distinct advantage.

A novice should not hesitate to ask his supplier whether

Mosaic hen, Red. The coloration of this variety is the direct result of its siskin ancestry.

Silver Agate Opal. Dilution of menanins is the significant characteristic of this white-ground variety.

the birds he has acquired will, in fact, form suitable breeding pairs. Breeders and dealers have adequate knowledge to help by giving advice.

If we embark on breeding canaries with the immediate intention of exhibiting our birds, we will do better to start off with fewer but better breeding pairs than to purchase a large number of low-quality breeding birds. To try and produce improved stock from poor strains is a waste of time. There is no need to buy show champions, but we should aim for stock qualifying as "good" so that we can be sure of above-average quality in our birds.

Wherever possible we should examine prospective purchases personally. If buying sight unseen cannot be avoided, detailed conditions of purchase should be agreed upon beforehand between buyer and seller. This can save a lot of trouble.

self green Yorkshire
nary. 2. A 10 week old
der Canary. 3. A
e green Border
nary. The standard for
gth set by the Border
ciers societies
cifies that the bird
st not exceed 5 ½
hes.

Red, Nonintensive.

Red Agate Melanin-pastel, Intensive.

Left: Different cages for different canary varieties. Most bird societies in Europe are ve specific as to the type of cage that can be used for each varie ty. *Below:* Although this is the most commonly sold nest box is *not* appropriate for canaries Canaries use nest pans made metal, earthenware, plastic or wicker. Canaries never go into closed box.

*Breeding
Cages
and
Accessories*

Very important in determining your breeding success will be the accommodations you provide for the breeding birds. The hens are best placed in a large flight cage. They are allowed to remain together, keeping each other company. For about six hens a cage with a length of 70 cm is adequate, although a bigger cage is of course to be preferred. The females should be given a good mixed diet, with an occasional bit of apple and—in a separate dish—nourishing soft food, a term applied to items of diet other than seed and greens. Care must be taken with greenfood during the winter months, as it is liable to cause gastric upsets. Fresh, clean

bath water is essential. On bright sunny days the bath vessel may be given to the hens also in the winter (assuming the birds are kept in a cold environment). It promotes a feeling of well-being and helps to keep the birds in good condition.

Of prime importance is that the canary hens spend the winter in a cold place. If we keep them in a warm room, the mating instinct awakens too early. The nights, during which the delicate young are of course not given any food, are too long and the days are too short in February for the newly hatched chicks to survive. For this reason anyone breeding his birds early must not only provide a source of heat (which, of course, is very important) but also—and this is equally vital—make sure the breeding cage or the room in which it stands is illuminated. Light is a very important factor in preparing birds for mating. Quite recently research has shown that the "internal clock" of all living creatures, but most especially of vertebrates, including of course our canaries, is regulated by light. The duration of daylight controls the annual cycle of our birds.

Cock birds, on the other hand, may be left in the warm living room. Where males are concerned it does not matter whether the pairing urge awakens earlier than is necessary. They need not be given the same rich diet as the hens. Ten parts of hemp and rape seed in equal amounts to one part of niger seed is perfectly sufficient. It is better to sprinkle the niger on top, pure, when the feeding trough has been filled with the hemp and rape mixture. In this way we avoid letting the male scatter too much food in his search for his favorite, the niger seeds. Apples, like other greenfoods, promote the studs' digestion and health. But if the cocks remain in a warm environment we need not worry about their digestion. The cock birds, too, should be offered a bathing dish at least twice a week.

If, like the hens, the studs spend the winter in cold rooms, we have to bear in mind that the cocks' testes will mature more slowly than the hens' ovaries. This frequently results in the production of "clear," or unfertilized, eggs. The production of such eggs has nothing to do with the sex drive of the birds! It merely indicates the absence of fully matured sperm.

Canaries that spend the winter in a cold environment should have their diet supplemented with vitamins; pet shops have many types available. It is not strictly necessary for the birds to spend the winter in really bright roooms, but the one-time practice of darkening the cages so that the birds lived in semi-darkness is a cruelty that should belong to the past.

The actual breeding cages, nowadays, are generally supplied in the dimensions 40 x 30 x 30 cm per breeding compartment. While breeding may be successful in this confined space, I regard these dimensions as quite inadequate. They remind me of conditions that prevail in modern chicken farms, where the (battery) hens have no room to move. Cages of 50 cm are considerably better; the birds can move much more easily inside them. The perches should be far enough apart for the birds to have to use their wings when "jumping" from one to the next.

Whether one uses box-type or metal cages for breeding depends on the circumstances and is a matter of personal preference. I have been using both kinds with equally good results for the last 20 years. For canaries highly stylized in shape and for the breeding of hybrids I prefer box-top models, cages with three solid walls. The birds feel more secure inside them and tend to be calmer than in open cages. In addition, there is a certain amount of protection against drafts. The perches must not be fitted too close to the ceiling of the cage or the stud will have difficulty in mounting the hen. He needs enough room to flap his wings, since he flutters them during copulation. This is especially important with regard to anyone breeding tall and large varieties for position. All too often beginners overlook this point and, when they subsequently find unfertilized eggs in the cage, do not realize they have only themselves to blame.

The food and water troughs must be fitted inside or to the breeding cage in such a way that changing or filling them does not disturb the birds. Anyone driving the hen off the nest every feeding time and having to remove the nest and then reach into the cage with his hand is unlikely to derive much pleasure from breeding canaries. All disturbances must be avoided if at all possible. There is nothing the birds need more during the breeding season than peace and quiet.

Whether the nest is inside or outside depends on the size of the cage and general arrangements. If the cage is very spacious there is little reason for having the nest on the outside. Breeders who set up a "community room" will prefer the nests to be inside.

Community breeding is a method dating back to the 1800's when it was practiced above all in the Harz Mountains. A big separate flight room is used to accommodate hens and studs for breeding in larger numbers. Usually there are three or more cock birds and four to five hens per breeding compartment. One disadvantage of community breeding is frequent disturbances. For contemporary breeders community rooms are without interest anyway, since it is impossible to determine the parentage of the young with certainty. Furthermore, the constant fighting in such an environment, caused by territorial defense and the ceaseless mating songs of the cock birds, is cruel to the animals. This form of breeding can be done sensibly and humanely only in very spacious aviaries.

Compared with community breeding, there is a lot to be said for the method by which a single stud fertilizes several hens in rotation and the hens are kept in individual cages and have to do all the work (nest-building, incubating, rearing) unaided. This method, however, is dismissed as unsuitable by modern breeding standards on account of its disadvantages for the chicks. It is justified only in certain exceptional cases, as for example, when an extraordinarily good stud is desired to pass on his unusually beautiful and valuable characteristics to as many offspring as possible. The hens are obliged to do all the rearing work by themselves, which means the chicks are fed by only one parent.

The best and at the same time most natural method of canary breeding is to provide one compartment for each pair of birds. The birds stay together all year long and raise their young together as well.

Many breeders of song canaries, even today, continue to believe in letting one stud serve three to four hens in rotation, and they practice what they preach. But those breeding their birds for color—and even more so the breeders interested in shape—think much more in accordance with Nature.

STARTING A CANARY FAMILY

When is the most favorable time to initiate breeding? When should stud and hen be put together? These are the two most burning questions for the novice. To reply to them by suggesting a specific date would be absurd. In Germany, the traditional date is St. Joseph's Day, the 19th of March. This is an old rule of thumb. However, breeders having heated rooms at their disposal generally can—or indeed must—start earlier than that. Once the birds are in breeding condition it would be a serious mistake to delay them. Their whole cycle would then be upset, and things rarely would run smoothly after that. The best time to start breeding is the end of March. At around the 20th of March or so the birds are put into the breeding cage, earlier if they themselves have unavoidably determined the date by their behavior!

The hen canaries grow restless and give their trilling mating call, usually delivered in a high-pitched voice. They are forever running about and flapping their wings.

Restlessly searching, they fly from perch to perch. At a later stage they usually take a feather into the beak (nest-building ceremony). Among themselves the females have become even more aggressive than they were before. Now is the time to put them into a breeding cage. The nest pan should be put in as well. From then on the hens are given a small quantity of "egg food," just enough to cover the point of a knife, every day.

This "egg food" plays a very important part in canary breeding. It serves as a supplementary food in the breeding season and is also employed as a rearing food for the young. Its name is derived from the most important ingredient: finely mashed hard-boiled hen's egg. To prepare this food, one egg is boiled for 10 minutes and shelled; it is then passed through a fine sieve or an egg press. It is then mixed with three tablespoons of rusk flour until it has the consistency of light, fine crumbs. Over this are sprinkled two teaspoons or less of poppy seeds, and that is all there is to it. Hundreds of thousands of canaries have been raised on this.

The breeder of today has ready-weighed raising mixtures at his disposal. In any case, few hobbyists can afford the time to prepare their own raising food. They rely on a commercial mix that contains all the nutrients the canary chicks require. There is a whole range of excellent reliable mixtures on the market. Not only the composition is important, however, but also the consistency. The food should be light and of a moist-to-crumbling consistency. Then it is just right for the beaks of the canary parents. It is vital that the food be neither wet nor forming sticky lumps. That would be dangerous for the chicks. On the other hand, if it is too dry the hens are not very keen on picking it up; it hinders the formation of mucus necessary before the food can be passed to the young. This varies from one hen to another, however, and the breeder is advised to adapt himself to the "personal preference" of his hens. Rule of thumb: better a bit on the dry side than too wet. Bird biscuit is a food of almost equal importance in canary breeding. It too can be bought ready to use; simply put it back into the cage in pieces of suitable size.

These rearing foods are given to the hens immediately after they have been transferred to the breeding cages. Use caution, however, if the temperature falls below 15°C., because egg food then causes slight gastric upsets. On such cold days a bit of dry biscuit is better. The same caution applies where greenfood is concerned: it had better not be administered at all on cold days, as it may then do more harm than good.

Do not provide too much nesting material at once. It would get dirty very quickly, and we can never be sure when the female actually starts building the nest. A few short threads of lint should suffice to tell us whether the hen is about ready.

The novice must never be impatient. Above all, breeders must not hold the mistaken belief that it is necessary "to do something" all the time. Constant interference almost invariably has fatal consequences. It is very important that the birds be allowed to pass through all the natural stages of breeding. The restless phase of "searching for a nest" (which for the caged canary is of course merely symbolical), pair-formation, deciding where to have the nest, nest-building and mating, the feeding of the hen by the cock bird, egg-laying, incubating, etc.—all these important events in the life of the birds must be allowed to proceed undisturbed and as naturally as possible. To interfere, if at any breeding stage things appear to have gone wrong, would be a grave error. For example, a hen that seems unenthusiastic about nest-building, or even totally uninterested in it, should be left alone by us. Giving a certain amount of help or providing her with a nest would be acceptable only if the hen had already started to lay. On no account must we remove everything, let alone take away the eggs, so that the hen is able to "start all over again."

This would upset the breeding cycle and, while we may sometimes be lucky and get away with it, it is an unnatural intervention and not advisable. The birds must be allowed the fullest possible freedom to live according to their instincts. If this is granted to them, there is the best possible chance that breeding will be successful.

If the stud has not been placed into the cage at the same time as his hen, he should be put in when nest-building has progressed to the stage at which the hen turns round while building. That is the best moment. Before then, fierce fighting may ensue. If the birds attack each other nonetheless, take the cock out again and put him back in at dusk in the evening.

Lint on its own tends to be disappointing as nesting material; it is too soft. Dry moss and soft, short grass (supplied in the early stages of nest-building) provide the nest with a firmer "frame." If we later on let the bird have lint for padding the interior, we get magnificently firm nests with a delicate, round hollow on the inside. Everyone who keeps canaries will be astonished to find what beautiful nests these birds can build.

The eggs are usually laid in the morning hours, around 7 or 8 o'clock. When straining to expel the egg the hen gets up and stands in the nest with her beak open. Afterwards she crouches down to recover from the exertion. We must not disturb her now. Later (not until noon) we take out the egg, preferably with a small spoon, and replace it with a dummy egg. The first egg and all subsequent ones, produced at the rate of one a day, of the same clutch are carefully stored in cotton wool or on sand until the final egg (which is smaller and usually differs in color as well) has emerged. The purpose of removing the eggs and then putting the whole clutch back into the nest simultaneously is to ensure that all the chicks hatch on the same day. Personally, I put the eggs back on the evening of the day the hen has laid her third egg. This method achieves good results. All four chicks—four is a good number for a successful brood—then hatch on the same day. One important point to remember is to remove the third egg at noon and let it cool off.

The incubation period of canary eggs is 13 days. Cool weather and disturbances may, if circumstances are really bad, extend it to up to 16 days. It is vital that we contain our curiosity during this time and leave eggs and hen undisturbed. The best hatching results can be expected after a period of 13 days. If the chicks hatch a day later, results still tend to be good. But if it takes longer than 14 days, we may have to prepare ourselves for complications. Young canaries hatch in the same way as, for example, young chickens. With the aid of a small protuberance (the "egg tooth") at the tip of the upper mandible, the young bird breaks open a tiny area of the egg shell from the inside. Then it starts to breathe and continues to break its way out. The small hole is enlarged, but not very much, before the chick makes the shell burst right across into two pieces. There is nothing, really, the beginner can do to help; to free a newly-hatched canary chick that is sticking to the egg membrane requires a lot of skill and experience.

AFTER HATCHING

Surely one of the loveliest experiences a breeder can have is to hear that thin tweet! tweet! from inside the nests, indicating that the young have hatched. On the day before hatching the thoughtful breeder should already have offered a little egg-food or biscuit to the hens, food they have been having to do without during the incubation period. It is advisable not to let the hens have too much food. If they get too much they might be "forced" into breeding again after far too short an interval. In their natural environment, birds are generally restricted in their food intake during the breeding season by their brood-caring duties.

The babies do not require any food on the day of hatching. They carry their own food supply in the form of the yolk sac, which on the babies' last day inside the egg is drawn inside the abdominal cavity. The yolk sac allows them to survive the first few hours of life. The yolk sac is perfectly sufficient for the first day. On the second day, however, we need to provide egg-food (raising food). From the fourth day onwards we supply fresh greenfood in addition, and it is astonishing how rapidly the young birds grow during the first few days of life. Their appetite and digestion match their growth rate. The bird mother keeps the nest interior scrupulously clean. The droppings of the chicks are encased in a thick bag of mucus and are picked up with the beak and removed just as soon as they have been produced. After about seven or eight days this "membrane" is no longer present. From then on the young search for the edge of the nest, push themselves up to it with the rear end and skillfully drop their excreta over the edge. Now is the time for close-ringing. Rings put on any earlier just get lost, and if the young birds are ringed too late their delicate feet get injured.

The task of feeding the chicks is shared by the parents. The stage of total dependence continues until the young are 16 days old. From the fourteenth day we must stop handling the nest in any way, as from then on the behavior of the young bird changes. Up to that time they crouch deep down inside the hollow of the nest and get as close to one another as possible when we take down the nest for checking or they feel the slightest vibration. But now the "flight instinct" (in the sense of escaping to safety) begins to awaken inside them. The young birds may then jump out of the nest in a blind panic when the menacing human comes towards them. To put a youngster that has escaped from the nest back in again would be pointless. After all, the young birds need to get to know their environment and how to move about in it. They need to learn to judge distances, for example. For this reason they flutter about at the wire mesh a lot during these critical days, behaving almost like wild birds. After two to three days they have come to understand what it's all about, and their movements are no longer aimless. In the breeder's eyes they now behave "sensibly."

THE FLEDGLINGS' FIRST EXCURSION

Canaries remain nestlings for 15 to 17 days. By the end of that period their plumage is almost complete. Only the fluffy down on the head and the stunted little tail give away their tender age. Their feathers are also more matte in color than are those of adult birds. As a rule, the strongest among the young birds is the first to leave the nest. Somewhat aimlessly it flutters about on the bottom of the cage and gives forth its begging cry. It soon learns to find its way around, however, and so of course do its siblings. During this time it is best to leave the young birds to their own devices. It is also a good idea to clean the cage when the chicks are about 12 days of age. In this way we avoid worrying the young when pulling out the drawer for cleaning. Equal care is required when feeding the young. We must make sure that we do not injure any of the clumsy little creatures. It is all too easy for them to get wedged in somehow or to get a toe caught in the wire.

The time of beginning independence is the most critical period for young birds. Their little beaks are still soft and delicate. They are not yet able to extract hard seeds from their husks, so we have to continue to provide rearing-food. The food is best served in a large trough on the bottom of the cage. (Ideally suited for the purpose are the dishes placed under flower pots.) Then the young birds can see their food better, and it also seems they enjoy their food more in company. The "egg-food" is now given to them dry and with less egg, and we gradually mix it with more and more crushed seeds. We prepare the seeds by distributing them between two sheets of paper and crushing them through the paper with a rolling-pin or a bottle. At least the majority of seeds will be crushed by this method, which provides a "coarse granulation" and is perfectly sufficient. In this way the young canaries slowly learn how to pick up seeds and how to remove the husks.

The sooner the young are now moved into their own quarters the better. By this time the mother usually feels a very strong urge to build a new nest, and she then plucks her own young. The light-colored smaller feathers are most in danger of being pulled out by her. This problem of plucking is a very widespread one among cage birds, a real plague. All breeders are faced with it. Responsible, of course, is the confined space in which we are forced to keep cage birds. This inevitably leads to exaggerated reproductive urges and hence to this type of abnormal behavior. In addition, however, the downy small feathers serve as a trigger for the function of gathering nesting material. More than 500 generations of cage breeding have obviously not been enough to eradicate this type of innate behavior, which is necessary in the wild but pointless in the cage.

NURSERY SCHOOL FOR BABY CANARIES

After 22 days we take the young canaries out of the breeding cage. They now go to "nursery school." That is, we put them into as spacious a cage as possible; there they can be looked after by the father or another reliable "nurse." In my case, a Norwich cock performed this baby-sitting task very satisfactorily for some years. Although the young birds are already able to pick up their own food, they do not eat enough at this stage. An experienced cock or hen can then carry on where the young leave off and feed them. Among my own birds, apart from the Norwich cock, there was also a female bullfinch who took it upon herself to look after the young canaries. She became expert, above all, at looking after "problem" youngsters. The young of canaries bred primarily for shape—breeds in which the young often are lethargic—did well in her care.

It is important that the food for the chicks at this time be less rich. We give them less egg but increasingly more seeds. In the past, breeders used to make do with giving steeped rape seeds to the young birds, but that is not a good food. A breeder who takes the trouble to prepare germinated food for his birds and gives it to them fresh offers them something much better. I have to point out, however, that in the warmer months germinated food tends to go sour very easily and then goes bad, leading to intestinal troubles in the young birds. The seeds of weeds gathered by the breeder himself are much preferred, and the birds find them easier to digest.

Bath-water (which we change daily) and drinking water must never be absent. Canaries love bathing. In the summer they should even be encouraged to bathe twice a day, especially when it is very hot. Plenty of exercise, whenever possible in fresh air (even in the rain), is equally essential for healthy development of the young birds.

At the age of five to six weeks, the young canaries begin their first molt. In these very young birds it is only a partial molt; only the small feathers are lost. Flight and tail feathers remain unchanged. A rich diet, as varied as possible, guarantees that by the end of the molting period the young birds have truly grown up. The young cock birds are now ready to start their training, assuming that they belong to a variety that is bred for song and that the birds are intended for exhibiting.

For the breeder of show birds the molt is an especially important time, since he is now able (by means of color-feeding) to determine the birds' appearance. The color formed at this stage will remain unchanged until the next molt.

It is essential that the birds do not have to live in cramped conditions during the molting period. No cage is too big, and the more exercise the young birds get the better. If kept in too small a cage, the young canaries frequently start plucking each other. This plucking is, however, nothing like the purposeful plucking performed by the mother who is getting ready for the next brood. Rather, it indicates a search for something to do—a playful tug at the neighbor that can become a habit or even a compulsion. Once a young bird has become "addicted" to the blood-filled quills he starts to make a terrible nuisance of himself among the young flock and needs to be isolated. I would not like to confirm unreservedly that the often-cited offering of a piece of sisal string to the bird through the bars does in fact divert his attention and effect a cure. Once again: not too many birds in the cage, a varied diet and plenty of bathing opportunities will provide sufficient prevention. Wild seeds, put into the cage in the form of whole fruits, keep the flock of youngsters occcupied. Any bird that has begun to exhibit the vice of feather plucking should be isolated without delay, before it has a chance to disfigure its companions. It is surprising how much damage these "adolescents" can do within a short period.

When no more "stubble" can be discerned on the heads of the young birds the process of molting has been completed. Now, at the age of about five to six months, the birds have become adults.

Canaries that have completed the process of molting look smooth and shiny. Bright eyes and an energetic, lively personality show us they are in good health. The young cocks now strive to perfect their song. A new chapter has begun in their lives.

At this point the breeder can decide which of the animals he wants to keep and which he is going to dispose of. For young cocks of the song varieties, the time has come to be segregated. Color varieties continue to occupy mixed quarters for a little longer. By the beginning of November, however, they too are segregated into males and females and moved to new quarters. Although the birds are already wearing their "wedding dress," it is necessary to keep the sexes apart.

PROBLEMS DURING INCUBATION

The breeding and rearing of canaries from the egg to the independent young bird takes about one month. During this period the birds have to perform a whole range of duties that are governed by complex biological processes. If any part of this complicated business goes wrong, other disturbances are sure to follow. It is important that the breeder interfere as little as possible. Hens that show a lack of interest in food should first of all be offered a variety of raising foods, apart from the obligatory egg-food: biscuit, dried grated rusk (pure), a little egg yolk (pure), chickweed with seed capsules or even ant pupae. Ant pupae promote the flow of crop mucus. Incidentally, we must never forget that canaries are individuals and have personal likes and dislikes. For this reason there is no fool-proof recipe for breeding. The true breeder has to have intuition, empathy and skill if he wants to be successful in the long term. These qualities can be acquired only by plenty of practice. No book can provide them—and no advice, however well-meant.

HAND-REARED YOUNGSTERS

It can happen that the parents stop looking after their brood, in spite of all our care and consideration, perhaps because of an overpowering urge to breed again. This happens particularly among the more highly stylized varieties. There can be no doubt that this is the result of the unnaturally favorable conditions that prevail in our cages. If the young birds are to survive, we either have to transfer them to other nests or else rear them by hand. Women are, by nature, much more skilled than men when it comes to rearing baby birds artificially. Even though the canary hen does not feed her chicks, we should nevertheless leave the

The youngsters in this Border Canary family are approximately eight weeks old.

1

2

3

young with her for a few more days. In practice this means that every couple of hours we take out the young (complete with nest) and feed soft food to them with the help of a wooden spatula. Usually the "food-provider" is greeted by greedily opened hungry beaks.

The simplest method of preparing food for hand-rearing is to mix egg-food with saliva. Lots of little birds have been successfully raised in this way. Human saliva is, however, not an ideal ingredient of canary food. Heavy smokers or anyone who is ill should refrain from preparing such a mixture. Nor should it be forgotten that saliva contains germs and bacteria. But currently these dangers tend to be over-emphasized (which is why I have mentioned this "old-established recipe" nonetheless).

Alternatively, lukewarm water can be used, and with equal success, although it makes the consistency of the food less perfect for the little beaks. It is very important, however, that the temperature be correct; the food should always be of body temperature.

Wherever possible, the cooperation of the bird mother should be utilized. The nest remains in or on the cage and is touched only when the young are being fed. At first the babies receive food every hour, later at longer intervals. The lining of the nest, absorbent muslin paper, should be replaced at least once a day.

1. Border Canaries. 2. A buff Border hen. 3. A baby Gloster Canary.

This two year old hen
(pictured left) was
awarded best white
in the Bristol C.B.S.
Show and best white
in the Welsh Border
Show. A variegated
buff Norwich is
shown below.

Canary
Varieties

The canary has been kept as a pet for roughly 500 generations now. In human terms this equals a period of 15,000 years. This comparison shows how extremely rapid the evolutionary history of the canary varieties has proceeded.

The culprit, of course, is our curiosity. For all these years we have constantly tried to add new varieties to the existing, familiar ones. Not only in respect of song did we seek to create variety but also with regard to appearance—that is, shape, color and plumage.

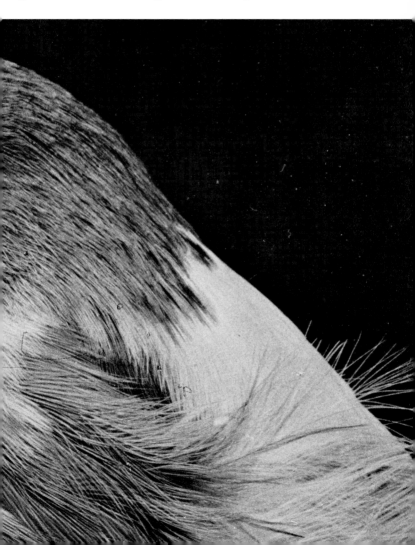

The birth of new races in the animal and plant kingdoms never happens out of the blue, as a sensational surprise; instead, it comes about as the result of a ceaselessly active "life-urge"—an urge for movement and change. "Everything flows," as the ancient Greeks used to say, meaning that nothing ever remains unchanged. Ever since there was life on this planet new forms of life have been evolving. This living process has now been going on for many millions of years on earth, and all creatures have been shaped by it. Function and advantage and relation to the environment have been the decisive factors. The term "evolution" has become the foundation pillar of biological thinking and stands for an accumulation of knowledge and ideas which benefit the breeder as well.

One characteristic of this flux is Nature's potential for sudden, spontaneous genetic changes. Such phenomena are called mutations. Needless to say, the occurrences of these sudden changes are of interest to breeders, who cultivate them in a special way. A knowledge of the genetic laws, as elucidated by the Augustinian monk Mendel over a hundred years ago, is an absolute must for the breeder. If we take the canary as an example, a whole range of genetic factors crucial in breeding are known. For a complete understanding of all these characteristics and their origins one would need a science degree.

This need not concern the hobbyist, however. He simply chooses a variety or color he likes and breeds with it. Gradually, as he gets deeper and deeper into the subject matter, he will acquire the necessary theoretical knowledge. What truly matters is the pleasure the hobbyist derives from working with birds regardless of how and on what scale he breeds his canaries.

CANARY COLORS
To the layman the multitude of splendid colors of all the different classes that confronts him at a canary exhibition

seems overpowering. Indeed, the canary can at present be bred in more than 500 different color varieties; 100 of them can be seen at bird shows. The remaining shades are less important, as their color effect is less marked. Only the easily recognizable colors are accepted and entered by the experts from the cage bird societies.

The confusing variety does not begin to make sense until we analyze each color for its main components. Broadly speaking, the color of a canary results from the following two groups:

1. Carotenoid pigments, or carotenoids (named after the pigment found in the carrot).
2. Melanins.

About these groups the canary fancier needs to know a bit more so that he is able to identify and work with them properly.

Carotenoids, in the past also known as lipochromes, are widely distributed in the plant kingdom. The canary has to take them into its system with the food. The body then transforms them into the specific colors that, in accordance with the bird's genetic make-up, characterize the canary concerned. In liquid form the colors are transported in the bloodstream to the quills of the feathers, where they crystallize in the keratinizing feather tissue. This process takes place only during the molting period, when the vascular feather papilla is still closed. As soon as the feathers have pushed through they contain their permanent carotenoid deposit. At the base, the depositing of pigments continues until keratinization has occurred.

In the canary, carotenoid pigments are present in the range yellow (canary xanthophyll) to fiery red (canthaxanthin). The wild canary's basic color is a natural yellow, while the fiery red variety owes its color to cross-breeding with the hooded siskin from Central America. This crossing-in is essential for all red canaries. It ensures that the color gene "R" (red) becomes securely anchored in the birds' hereditarty material, thus enabling them to transform suitable plant substances into the red carotenoid "canthaxanthin." This synthesis takes place primarily in the liver. I must add, however, that only healthy birds that are given fresh plants in sufficient quantities at regular intervals are able to achieve uniform coloring. Optimal feeding of red color varieties during the molt is therefore of the greatest importance.

Where the white canaries are concerned, mutations have prevented the visible deposition of carotenoid pigments. Today there are two white varieties. In one the white color is dominant, whereas in the other it is recessive in relation to the normal carotenoid ones.

Melanins occur naturally in a canary's body and do not depend on food intake. (However, that the birds must receive a normal diet and enjoy good health goes without saying.) They are the most widespread pigments in the bird world and range from sand-yellow to jet black. Breeders refer to them all as dark colors.

Biologically, melanin synthesis is a fairly complex process. It proceeds via a number of intermediate products with the aid of specific hormones (tyrosinase-dopa) to the end products (eumelanin and phaelomelanin). What the dark colors look like is, further, influenced by mutations concerning melanin density and type and feather structure. A piebald appearance is caused by the localized absence of melanin and is well known to us with regard to all domestic animals. The complete absence of melanin pigment is collectively described as "albinism" by biologists. In the canary, however, the carotenoids can—independently of this—produce coloration. But in such cases the eyes remain unaffected and the blood vessels are, therefore, visible and make them look red. Red eyes, incidentally, are always indicative of albinism; they provide a simple way of spotting the condition.

A third, although much less important, group are the

structural colors. They rarely occur in the canary, however.

The optical "blue" factor results from a characteristic cell change in the feathers. It turns a normal yellow canary into a lemon-yellow bird. An ordinary slate-gray bird becomes a "steel-blue" bird. In red factors the bird's color appears more intense.

Then there is the "opal factor," influencing the melanin appearance, and a "structural carotenoid factor," which influences the carotenoid appearance. The latter factor is referred to as the "lipochrome-pastel factor" by German breeders. Nomenclature and gene symbols have yet to be internationally agreed upon.

LIGHT-COLORED BIRDS

The main characteristics of all light-colored varieties are white flights and tail, which show at most a narrow carotenoid margin. The contour feathers are yellow to red in all sorts of intermediate shades from orange-yellow to orange-red. The carotenoid pigment is deposited in the feathers in liquid form, as already mentioned, and the proportion of yellow and red also flows in all the different blends without shading. For convenience and reasons of nomenclature the breeders have divided up this flow into distinguishable color classes marked with Roman numerals I to V on the color scale used. Where the feathers contain no carotenoid pigment whatsoever we get a bird with a white basic color. This applies to the recessive white canaries, for example. Conversely, dominant whites still show some carotenoid pigment on the tips and the bends of the wings.

The best-known canary is the yellow kind. It arose with the loss of melanin pigments found in the green, wild form. If the optical "blue-factor" is present, the yellow becomes a lemon-yellow, while the much sought-after gold yellow variety possesses a double "intensive factor." The intensive factor is connected with the more magnificent plumage of males. The nonintensive canaries are associated with the plainer-looking females, as is generally the case with birds of the finch family.

This characteristic refers only to the carotenoid colors, which may show a third variation in addition to the two already mentioned—namely the "mosaic" color, as it is known in German, or dimorphic color in English. In this variation only certain areas show carotenoid coloring: eyestripe, "elbow" and tail. In additon there is a carotenoid sheen on the breast. These typical carotenoid markings are exhibited only by the females and can also be seen in the hens of the original species, the serin finch and hooded siskin. Their feathers show the same distribution of carotenoid color.

To measure the carotenoid colors more precisely, breeders use a comparative plate with color samples after Oswald's standard tables. With reference to the canary, the section between 1 and 6 has been divided up into quarters of a degree to form a measuring device. The carotenoid color can also be expressed in abbreviated form: "OF" ("Oswaldsche Farbnorm" which translates to "Oswald's color standard"). The Roman numeral of the color class in the international color table corresponds with the "OF" value as expressed in whole numbers.

The distinction between intensive (A) and nonintensive (B) refers not only to the color of a bird, but also to its plumage and its build. Intensive canaries are generally weaker and their plumage sparser or thinner. B-birds are heavier, their plumage thicker and fuller. The color in these birds looks as though it were covered with frost—hence the apt English term "frosted." This "coat of mold" is quite distinct and makes the color look paler (other English terms are "mealy" and "buff").

DARK-COLORED CANARIES
AND AGATE CANARIES

The wild canary is green. Its green coloration results from the presence of yellow carotenoids and blackish brown melanin pigments. Due to careful selection, the domesticated dark-colored variety has already been moving in the direction of "pure, deep black." The main characteristics of the dark-colored variety are dark flights and tail, dark legs and claws and a dark beak. Ideally, legs, claws and beak should be black. In Oswald's color table these birds form color group 2. The five different color classes in combination with undiluted black melanins are: *Green,* in the shades lemon and gold; *Bronze:* orange-yellow carotenoid; *Copper*-colored: orange carotenoid; *Copper-red*-colored: orange-red carotenoids; *Red-black:* red carotenoid. In combination with a white basic color (carotenoids are completely absent) we have the slate-colored variety.

"Agate" birds show, instead of black melanins, a grayish anthracite-colored pigmentation. The microscopically small color granules are present only at half their usual density in these birds; in other words, the melanin has been "diluted." Characteristic for agate canaries are prominent markings on the head. These markings consist of a carotenoid stripe above the eye and a dark-colored agate "beard" and resemble those of the Mozambique serin finch. The horny parts, beak, legs, feet and claws are of a light lead-gray color. "Dilute melanin" is a hereditary sex-linked recessive characteristic. The gene for this character is located on the sex chromosome, for which reason it can be carried as a masked trait by some cocks. Externally these cocks are virtually indistinguishable from dark-colored ones. Among the females there are no heterozygous agate birds. A canary hen is always homozygous for the melanin density and type (black or brown) she exhibits.

Those birds belonging to color group 3 are described by the term "agate" followed by the color name from group 2.

Birds with a white basic color form an exception; they are referred to as "silver agate." Agate birds are popular varieties with a considerable sponsorship.

BROWN BIRDS AND ISABEL BIRDS

Brown birds have evolved from the original dark-colored birds, which, of course, still show a brownish black pigmentation. The brown pigments have broken away from the black ones and are alone now visibly deposited in the feathers. Again it is the flight and tail feathers that show the characteristic brown coloration most prominently. It is a warm fawn-color; depending on the amount of red mixed into it, it can be intensified into a rich coffee brown. In birds with an "undiluted" melanin pigmentation (this applies to both dark-colored and brown birds) the striations of the shafts must be broad and long yet straight and in line with the vanes. The color groups of birds with a "diluted" melanin pigmentation, agate and isabel, should show a shorter pigmented shaft portion in the contour feathers. This results in characteristic markings that are reminiscent of the back-stitch on a quilt. The striations must in every case be interrupted, yet straight and in line with the vanes, just as in the black and brown varieties.

Now to nomenclature. Brown birds are called by the color names of the light-colored birds, except that the syllable "brown" is added at the end. Brown birds with a white basic color are, however, described as "silvery brown." In a few cases, where color variations are concerned, the names given to the birds can only be referred to as verbal monstrosities or contradictions in terms. However, the individual color names have become so firmly established among breeders that it would be very difficult to introduce any revisions.

Isabel birds have very pale light brownish beige flight and tail feathers. This makes their carotenoid pigmentation almost as prominent as in light-colored birds. The striations are only very faintly visible and virtually absent on the flanks. The color effect varies with the red content. Isabel birds which look too brown, or indeed gray, are invariably the product of cross-breeding with other melanin groups. They are regarded as faults.

PASTEL COLORS

There can be no doubt that the choice of German nomenclature is not always too happy where color canaries are concerned. A particularly unfortunate term is "pastel." Two entirely different characteristics are called "pastel" by German and English breeders. One is a structural change of the feather, which alters the appearance of the carotenoid pigmentation. By the Dutch, in whose country this characteristic occurred as a mutation in 1950, this is described as "Ivoor" (ivory) and has been given the symbol "sc" (structural carotenoid factor).

This factor makes the carotenoid pigments look as though they had been covered with frosted glass. The resulting color shades look delicate and glazed and shine like enamel. This interesting color character, initially occurring in clear birds and bred into the whole range 1 to 5 on the Oswald scale, is now being introduced into a great many melanin groups as well. We therefore get a multitude of new colors. In Germany these birds are called "lipochrome pastels."

The second type of pastel birds, also referred to as such in other languages, are called "melanin pastels" in German and Dutch. This mutation (which also originated in Holland, from an isabel variety) softens the dark colors and makes them look "veiled." This veiled effect is seen above all on the back. As a result of chromosome-separation after synapsis (crossing-over), all four of the "classic melanin groups" can already be seen with the pastel factor. In Italy especially, the more recent color blends with pastel factor have triggered off a great new fashion trend in breeding circles. The factor is at its most beautiful in combination with brown pigments. In black-colored birds it produces a delicate brownish hue that does not go with the color type. Nonetheless, because of the fashion trend, these new creations always arouse a good deal of enthusiasm among breeders, which in turn promotes healthy ambition and canary-breeding of a high standard.

OPAL CANARIES

Opal canaries developed as a mutation from a green song canary variety near Furth in southern Germany. They turned up in the early 1950's and were simply called "Further agate canaries" because they bore a faint resemblance to the "classic" agate birds. As opposed to the classic agate characteristics, however, the opal factor is passed on freely and independently by all classic melanin groups. Depending on color group, opal birds vary considerably in appearance. "Undiluted" dark-colored birds of color group 2 show a lead-gray/bluish coloration of the large feathers while the horny parts—beak, legs, feet and claws—have remained as dark as they were. In agate birds the striations have been greatly reduced, and all the markings become considerably less conspicuous. In combination with brown pigment the opal factor does not look very attractive. In isabel birds with the opal factor the dark coloration has been so weakened that barely any remnants of markings are visible. Dark birds without markings are produced. Interesting though the opal birds are, breeding experiments with every possible combination are not advisable. For the breeder who wants to be well acquainted with the hereditary material of his breeding stock it is essential to have considerable knowledge and to keep strictly accurate breeding records. However, if one is hard-working and thorough in one's approach one may well be rewarded with the occasional stroke of luck. The "gray-winged" birds that have recently become known, for example, are the result of such combination experiments with the opal factor. Incidentally, one characteristic expression of the opal factor is that the feathers look bluish only on top, while the underside has remained dark.

COLOR COMBINATIONS

The "gray-winged birds" just mentioned, the "Viola-canarini" of the Italians (a very recent creation), the "Rose-ivoor Opal" and "Bronce-ino-ivoor" of the Dutch—all these new varieties are merely the result of combining various characters that together are united in the same hereditary material. To achieve such color blends we need a lot of experience, patience and determination, for no one can predict whether plans of that nature will in fact succeed. The breeder who is interested in carrying out such experiments must have accurate breeding records to fall back on. Without the records he cannot possibly see how his new creations have come about. The goal of all breeding experiments is a result that is capable of reproducing itself. A chance hit, with no hope of a repeat, is of little use.

A few possible combinations with "the latest" mutations: "Dilute" dark-colored birds (agate) with lipochrome pastel and melanin pastel; "Dilute" dark-colored birds with lipochrome pastel and opaline; "Dilute" brown birds (isabel) with lipochrome pastel and melanin pastel. All these color shades benefit from a high red content. A number of well known breeders are already devoting their attention to such creations and selling their "hits" as well.

The combination of dark pigment and melanin pastel resulted in the "gray wings" metioned above, whose pinions have a "margin" which shows up as a "band" in the wing.

The lipochrome pastel coloration is, of course, also bred in combination with birds having a yellow basic color. The colors resulting from this have a delicately glazed appearance which the experts find very appealing.

Many lay people, I regret to say, still hold the mistaken belief that the term "color canaries" always refers to red canaries or, more generally, red-factor birds regardless of which color group they belong to. The range of canary colors that can be produced naturally is, in fact, much wider. Whatever the experiments decided upon, however, it is important to choose either light-colored birds (color group 1) or dark-colored birds (color groups 2 to 5). Crossing these two main categories with each other results in uncontrollable color distribution: patchiness. Only very experienced breeders are able to recognize and use to advantage such patterns as may exist within an intentional patchiness.

FRILLED CANARY VARIETIES
THE PARISIAN FRILL (Frise Parisien)
With a length of more than 20 cm, the Parisian Trumpeter is the biggest of all canary varieties existing today. "Fireworks of feather bunches" is an apt description of the bird's appearance. The bird is sprouting and sparkling all over; animated, daring "hair-styles" envelop the giant. It is a historic variety, well known and popular in Paris for a long time. For over a hundred years there has been a society in existince in its native city that is exclusively concerned with breeding this bird. There is no region of its body for which standards of feather style have not been set. This starts on the head and ends with the tail. The Parisian Frill enjoys great popularity not only in France but also in England, Belgium, Holland, Germany and Switzerland. In Italy and Latin America it is the favorite among all canary varieties.

Breeding this bird is not easy. Due to strict selection, which inevitably means inbreeding, the Parisian Frill is no longer as fertile as other canary varieties. Nor is the Parisian Frill a reliable parent; many breeders, therefore, use "nurses" to rear the young. Not everyone may approve of such methods, but there can be no doubt that they serve their purpose. In Italy and Brazil we now find real Parisian Frill giants of no less than 24 cm in length. The size of such imposing birds is, of course, mainly the result of the thick plumage and the length of the feathers. These frills are roughly twice the size of the original form from the Canary Islands. A pinion (one of the longest tail feathers) measures a good 12 cm and is thus of the same size as a whole serin finch.

When breeding these giants it is best to provide separate compartments for each pair. The cage should be at least 70 to 80 cm long, and the perches must not be so high as to inhibit copulation. A nutritious diet is essential. Biscuits and other nourishing foods should be given to these birds the whole year 'round. Frilled canaries do not necessarily need a bath dish; they quite appreciate a going-over with the flower spray, and in this way their "locks" are not disturbed so much.

The food containers for all these artificial shape canaries should be spacious and designed like longish troughs so that the birds can see all their assorted edibles nicely spread out before them.

THE DUTCH FRILL

With its size of 17 to 18 cm the Dutch Frill comes somewhere between the Parisian Frill and the Belgian Frill (or Southern Dutch Frill) varieties in size. Its posture is straightly erect; its legs are almost straight too. The erect posture, a characteristic of all frilled canary varieties, brings out the full elegance of these birds. Frilled canaries are pure luxury creatures that feel happier in the cage than in the aviary. Also, to have their flight musculature too strongly developed would detract from their looks—the "stance" would suffer. To meet the standards, Dutch Frills have to have their feather-dress divided into three regions known as the *mantle* (the feathers on the back), the *jabot*

Red Agate, Intensive.

Green, Nonintensive.

(chest feathers) and the *fins* or supporting feathers (the long feathers sweeping upwards from the thighs). Often we find that the original French terms are still used with regard to these canaries, terms coined to suit the playful forms of a past epoch. The rococo school with its preference for curved arabesques and useless ornamentation has shaped the canary, too—the feathers curl inwards like shells.

The main characteristic of the Dutch Frill is the perfectly straight head-back-tail line. The color is immaterial where these canaries are concerned; they are judged purely for shape. Yet while no marks are awarded for color, the breeders of this variety in particular have shown a great interest in all the natural canary colors. Today we get these birds not only in yellow, green, cinnamon (brown) and white but also in slate, silvery brown, orange to red and even in isabel. Isabels appeared early among the Dutch Frills. These early reports do not refer to "dilute" brown birds, however, but simply browns. The melanin-diluting factor occurred and became known only at a later stage. When breeding shape varieties, and most particularly the highly artificial Frills, each pair of birds should be given its own breeding compartment. The Dutch Frill is a fairly hardy and healthy bird, probably holding the best chances of success for the beginner. Both sexes are dutiful parents. As for all the large varieties, however, the nest should be somewhat more spacious than for normal canaries. An area of 10 to 11 centimeters square would not be too big. The sides should be of adequate height as well. What must be regarded as a close relative, the older Frise de Picard, will be practically extinct by now. This bird was bred in the previous century in Picardie in France. It was a more original/primitive frilled variety.

THE BELGIAN FRILL
OR THE SOUTHERN DUTCH FRILL
The grotesque long-legged figure, the odd, unnaturally

hunched posture and the delicate, thin little head on the long neck—these characteristics of the Southern Dutch Frill do not appeal to every bird fancier. But, then, not every dog-lover finds the Italian whippet attractive, and not every pigeon breeder appreciates male pouter pigeons or peacock pigeons. The breeding of domestic pets has resulted in many examples of strange forms and shapes. It is not, after all, the purposeful adaptation to the environment, which in free Nature makes animals develop just so and no different, that sets the goals and standards here but purely and simply the "play-drive" of the breeders. They like their breed more enthusiastically than any other. Among the fanciers of these fantastic shapes are true artists and masters of their speciality. And, indeed, how else would it have been possible to evolve a creature of such perfection, a creature that looks like a sculpture from a studio of the "belle epoque"? About a hundred years ago a variety from northern France, "the Frise de Roubaix," became the ancestral contributor to many another breed of "hunched" Frill. The Munich, Swiss and Viennese Frill have all originated from this particular breed. The Viennese Frill really existed more on paper than in reality. The Swiss Frill was found in the Basle area, particularly at the turn of the century. A stronghold for Frills developed in Munich at the beginning of the century. About three hundred cages with Frill Canaries were exhibited there in the hey-day of the specialist society. Centrally kept breeding records ensured that the standards were strictly maintained. Unfortunately, a lot of valuable material was lost during the two world wars and changes in taste, and only very recently have there been reports of successes again which remind one of the best of those palmy days. In northern France the Frill is hardly kept at all nowadays. Only very occasionally may one come across an individual breeder who still does. This means that, in France at least, the best days of the frill are over, since stock of the highest quality

Silver-brown phaeo-ino.

This canary (pied) is the most common canary you can purchase in a pet store.

can be achieved only by breeding as many animals as possible and selecting the best. In Germany the interest in the frilled varieties is on the increase again. In Holland, on the other hand, Frill breeders are practically non-existent today.

FRILLED REGIONAL VARIETIES

The Swiss Frill is on the way back—the elliptical bird with the curvature of William Tell's bow has managed a come-back in its country of origin. It adopts the typical posture of all curved Frill varieties—firmly straightening itself out by raising the shoulders and extending the neck well forward. At the same time the head is pulled down, making head and neck come forward in a horizontal line. The best Munich Frill used to be excellent at doing this. The Swiss Frill does not pose quite to the same extent as the pure Southern Dutch Frill does today. It keeps its head up, as befits a member of the Swiss Confederation.

The Japanese have been breeding their own version of the Frill for 30 years, calling it *Makige*. What matters where these canaries are concerned is leg distance, ensuring that the frilled abdominal region comes fully into its own. The whole underside of the bird is required to be "styled." Very good birds have three lines of curls running downwards. The head should be small and the neck short. Considered to be the most attractive style for the back is a "flower," similar to the "bouquet" of the Parisian Frill. The legs are virtually straight. As regards some characteristics, the Japanese breed is the exact opposite of the varieties known in Europe, but the Japanese breeders work strictly in accordance with the high standards they have set themselves. In other words, the best *Makige* are high-class animals of no less significance than the best birds from other varieties. It is merely a matter of getting to know them, these curious canary shapes from distant Japan.

In Italy there exist three sub-varieties of the Parisian Frill adapted to suit local taste. In the Padua region breeders have created a large crested Frill. In Milan and surrounding areas a Color Frill has been bred, among the best specimens of which the white canaries in particular deserve to be mentioned here, as they boast the longest feathers and the thickest plumage.

THE GIBBER ITALICUS

The Gibber must be the oldest frilled variety in the world. It is not just its small size of about 15 cm that makes it different from the other representatives of this group. "Strip-tease canary" is a friendly nickname that points to the peculiarities of this breed. Its naked chest and thighs indicate that it needs a warm environment. Its posture must be permanently hunched to such a degree that the head never rises above the shoulders. Birds of this breed shown at exhibitions are invariably yellow specimens. The sparse plumage underlines the delicate bone structure of the bird still further. Its legs are perfectly straight. Occasionally one may see a bird whose joints are at a slight forward angle. While the Gibber's plumage, too, is divided into three parts, the individual regions are but sparsely feathered and without volume. It is astonishing how these little birds "perform" when requested to do so. "Performing" here refers to adopting the characteristic posture. That birds bred for shape cannot maintain their peculiar "standard position" continuously goes without saying. Their weird postures are, after all, not due to skeletal deformity but to muscular effort. Nor would a fair judge expect each and every bird that stands before him to instantly adopt the characteristic posture. Just as in weight-lifting the dumbbell need only be lifted into the correct position and held there for a very brief period, so the shape canary too need only "pose" briefly. On the other hand, the bird that performs more often and for longer is invariably regarded as

1

1. and 4. Paris frill. 2. North Hollander (piebald slate). 3. Gibber Italicus (below).

2

3

4

the better bird, by breeders and judges alike.

Occasionally some strange opinions are expressed as to how the remarkable posture of the frilled canaries might be achieved. There is talk, for example, of specially constructed rotating perches that were connected to each other by rope transmission and said to have been the secret of breeders from Munich in particular. In the same way one hears it whispered that "secret cages"—completely darkened and closed, apart from small holes at the appropriate level through which the birds can stick their heads to get at the food troughs hanging on the outside of the cage—are used. All these are fairy tales, but breeders have been known to believe in them nonetheless; perhaps they have even tried to put them into practice, thereby torturing the birds.

Neither in Munich nor in any other breeding center have these birds ever been subjected to such cruel, foolish techniques. This is most certainly not how the desired standard is achieved. Only selective breeding, together with staying-power and patience when training the birds, has ever led or is ever likely to lead to success.

A comparison can be made with certain breeds of the pigeon and chicken fanciers. There, too, curious shapes and postures were created as desirable fancy pieces. Only the variablility of the animal (and of plants, too) within domestication makes such "sport" possible. Many a zoologist talks about "perverting the natural creature," but man will always strive for what he does not yet possess. Thus the animals in his care will always be subject to new modifications, to whatever extent Nature cooperates.

CRESTED VARIETIES

Apart from the Crested Paduan, which belongs to the frilled varieties, three crested varieties are recognized as independent breeds today. These are the Crested Canaries of German origin, probably the oldest crested variety, and the two British breeds, the Crested Canary and the dwarf breed Gloster Fancy. The three differ so markedly in appearance that even the less experienced canary-keeper can readily tell them apart.

The German crested variety is in no way out of the ordinary in respect to either body shape or size. We can also describe it as the Color Crest, since the major breeding goal (after the crest, of course) is the bird's color. In shape, this breed resembles the Belgian Canary; it is, therefore, slightly larger as well as more upright than the German song canaries of the Roller breed. With a size of 14 to 15 cm, the German Crest comes exactly between the two crested varieties from Great Britain.

The British Crested Canary is exactly like the Norwich in form and size, although the two breeds are in no way related. It is incorrect to talk of the "Crested Norwich," for the ancestor of this massive, heavy canary variety is the Manchester Coppy (Lancashire breed) which unfortunately has become extinct. Breeding exclusively for long feathers leads very close to the limits of what Nature says is possible. The Crested is prone to the dreaded ailment known as "lumps," which are morbid growths on wings, chest or back and flanks. These cysts need not alarm us in every case; often they dry up and can then be removed. But such birds should never be used for beeding. If it cannot be avoided, then we must make sure to mate them only to a yellow partner.

The charming little Gloster Fancy has become the most widely distributed of all form varieties. It has a short and thick-set body; that is, it should look "chunky." Round all over and adorned with a bold "corona," it is always alert and full of life. Its proverbial good breeding properties and the devoted and reliable way in which it looks after eggs and young make the Gloster suitable for everyone, including the beginner, wishing to breed for form.

The canary crest is a mutation that occurred quite early.

1. Red, Intensive. 2. and 3. Gloster fancy coronas. 4. The head of a Gloster fancy. Because of the markings, this kind of crest is known as a "grizzled corona."

2

3

4

It has already been known for at least two hundred years, although for a long time it was treated as a variation, not as a breed in its own right.

THE NORWICH CANARY

The solid, heavy figure of the Norwich birds attracts the wonder and attention of all show visitors. The beautiful, perfectly rounded contours of this British breed and its confidingly tame behavior are what make it so desirable. Looking at the build of this bird, which is bred purely for shape, one could describe it thus: a pigeon's egg (head) sitting on a goose's egg (body). The most beautiful neck of the Norwich is no neck, as the breeders say, meaning that the structure of the head is a main characteristic of this breed; that is, the head should be broad and strong and, without any transition, should widen straight into the oval shape of the trunk. The feathers of the Norwich birds are long and of silky softness and evelop the birds smoothly all over. To ensure that their thick plumage is always immaculate and smooth, the Norwich Canaries need good care and attention, and their cages must be scrupulously clean at all times.

When breeding these birds each pair should be allocated a separate compartment, as applies to all large birds bred for shape. Norwich cocks make unusually touching husbands and fathers and do their utmost to look after hen and young. When they are to be mated it is a good idea to trim the small feathers around the cloaca a little.

The Norwich is of a quiet and placid disposition. In fact, the birds tend to be somewhat phlegmatic. For this reason it would do no harm to let them share their cage with a lively companion. I always place a cock from a color variety in the cage with them—except, of course, during breeding periods. When incubating, they are often too heavy for the newly-hatched young, and accidents are not uncommon. A big glass marble put into the nest helps with this problem. For many years, when my young Norwiches became independent, I placed a Peking robin in the flight cage with them and allowed this arrangement to continue until after the molt. The Peking robin served the purpose of "trainer." His very lively nature and aggressive stabs with the beak kept the horde of fatties on the wing. This proved an excellent technique. That the cage must be big enough to give the animals a chance to get out of each other's way goes without saying. A meter-long cage should never house more than eight or, at the utmost, ten birds. Important, too, is that the perches be sensibly arranged, allowing for adequate flight space and jumping opportunities. The perches should vary in thickness.

THE YORKSHIRE CANARY

Slender and upright, the plumage absolutely smooth all over and having a length of 18 cm, this bird is the "gent of the fancy" in England. This variety is not as old as the Norwich. It has been in existence for about a hundred years and owes its creation not only to Norwiches but also to Belgian Canaries and the Lancashire.

Once it was a narrow, thin little bird, but today when assuming its characteristic "carrot" shape, straightening itself and going into position, it is quite a giant among the diverse canary varieties. If the Yorkshire is to be exhibited, it requires a specific training that makes it go into the correct parade rest position expected of this variety. To be really handsome, a Yorkie must have long, almost extended legs. The quality of the plumage is judged as critically as a correct wing and tail carriage. The head-back-tail line must be absolutely straight. In England, concessions are now being made in the "wren-tail" direction. On the Continent, however, breeders have so far remained faithful to the more elegant version of the Yorkshire. At the turn of the century the ideal was that a pure-bred Yorkshire Canary had to pass through a man's wedding ring. Today the bird has not only

1

1. Clear yellow Yorkshire hen. 2. Norwich (buff). The head of the Norwich is somewhat flattened. 3. Yorkshire Canary. This one is a blue variegated white with eye and wing markings.

become heavier but longer as well. Nature allows herself to be shaped by man only up to a point. When that limit has been reached Mother Nature does what she, not man, thinks fit. The case of the Yorkshire Canary and its development over the last 50 years or so is a case in point.

THE BORDER FANCY

If we describe the Yorkshire as being "of noble birth," then the Border Fancy belongs to the "landed gentry." There is nothing spectacular about its shape or position. Of all varieties bred for position it is the one that bears the greatest resemblance to the normal canary. It does not stand very tall, yet it looks like a porcelain statue. Color, plumage, an absolutely trusting, tame nature, a beautiful curved outline—these are the characteristics every breeder wants to see. The Border Fancy occurs in all colors without red. It is a great delight to everyone who appreciates simple, natural beauty. There is no reason why this bird should not be bred by the beginner, too. Thanks to the popularity of this variety among breeders, specimens should remain readily obtainable at a modest price. The modern type is somewhat heavier than the old one, so a length of up to 15 cm has become acceptable.

THE BELGISCHE BULT CANARY OR BOSSU BELGE AND THE SCOTCH FANCY

These two varieties have a number of characteristics in common. Let us, therefore, note what distinguishes them from one another. The Belgian is the "angular" bird, while the Scot can be recognized by its circular shape. The Belgian Canary is a fairly old breed that nearly became extinct between the wars. It is now staging a fantastic comeback in its native country. The highest point of this bird, when the typical stance has been adopted, is the shoulder. The shoulder-tail line has to describe a sharp drop. The legs are firmly straightened and they, too, must stand vertically on the firmly closed feet. In the main, this variety is bred in pure yellow. The most handsome specimens are invariably yellow birds. The position, however, is equally good in buff specimens.

The Scotch Fancy is not widely distributed on the Continent as yet. Its legs are held tightly flexed, but this bird too pulls the head forward and even downwards while lifting the shoulders and "standing to attention." At the same time the tail is pressed towards the perch, as seen in the Belgian Frill. The Scotch Fancy is available in many colors. The color is immaterial, however; the one and only point of importance is that the bird instantly goes into action when requested to. "A Scot who does not work is not worth his food," as the saying goes. For a long time these oddly shaped canaries were held in great contempt in Germany and had to put up with a lot of abuse. Today, however, they have found a small number of supporters. It is not easy to raise an adequate selection of young birds for exhibition. Often it is necessary to enlist the help of foster parents, which does not appeal to everyone. The fancier who takes pleasure in unusual shapes will find these birds eminently suitable pets.

THE LIZARD CANARY

The feathers of this canary variety indeed look "scaly" and "lizard-like." Every one of the contour feathers has a light, bleached-looking margin. The Lizard is an old breed, a distinct mutation, and is unique among the canaries. It is bred for neither shape nor color, so it does not belong in any existing category. This explains why it is classified differently in different countries. The bird was named in Lizard-breeding land, England, and English terms are still internationally applied where sub-varieties and specific characteristics of the breed are concerned.

Instead of the terms "yellow" (A) and "buff" (B), we continue to say "gold" and "silver" when referring to the

1   2   3

4

1. Blue Lizard Canary. 2. Golden Lizard Canary. 3. Belgian Bult (Bossu belge). 4. Healthy looking canary family. 5. Border Fancy canary.

Lizard. The lighter-colored top of the head, which can make the bird look very attractive, is simply called the "cap." Its characteristic scales are known as "spangles," and the less well-developed scales on the underside are described as "rowings." The cap is not of the greatest importance, however; first come the spangles. And something else: the most beautiful Lizard is the black one! Flights, tail, beak, feet, legs, and claws—all must be jet black. The birds now also exist in brown melanin and agate. A number of breeders are striving to transmit the hereditary red factor of pure color birds to the Lizard Canaries. The feathers of the Lizards are slightly stronger in structure than those of color canaries. This makes the body appear stronger and fuller, too. What we know as blue Lizards are birds with a white basic color in dominant slate. They must always be paired to birds of another color, since crossing white with white means that this hereditary factor will have a lethal effect on 25% of the expected young (usually on the embryo inside the closed egg).

More nourishing food, such as that given to the large varieties, will do the Lizard Canaries no harm. Niger seed should not be missing from the menu and is preferably given pure in a separate trough. My Lizards used to sing but little. These birds are late developers; ideally they should not be mated until they are at least ten months old. Most judges who do not breed this variety themselves award too few points for them. The demands made on the Lizards are very high.

THE BERNESE CANARY

The capital of Switzerland has created its own canary variety. The Bernese bird with its smooth feathers is bred for shape and bears some resemblance to the Yorkshire variety from Britain. Someone who is not familiar with the Bernese Canary can confuse the two. However, the Bernese has a "square" flattened head, and its neck is constricted and of medium length. The wrist is held slightly away from the midline so that it becomes distinct from the outline of the body. The birds maintain an upright, raised posture. The joints of the legs are not quite straightened. With a size of 16 to 17 cm, the Bernese is slightly smaller than the Yorkshire. This variety has a fearless, challenging nature.

The Bernese Canary is of a uniform pure yellow; small patches are seen only rarely. Mottled, let alone dark, birds are not permitted. In the native city of this variety a special society endeavors to preserve and perfect this genuine Swiss creation, which came into existence at about the turn of the century. It was first exhibited in 1908.

THE MUNICH CANARY

This canary belongs to the group of smooth-feathered varieties bred for shape and stance. Like the Bernese, the Belgian and the Scotch Fancy, it has its greatest support in its actual place of origin. Developed after World War I, the creation of this breed was more an emergency solution than anything else. A lot of breeding material had been lost in the war, and stocks of the Munich Dutch were low. The studs therefore, were paired with ordinary canaries in an attempt to obtain an elegant, upright, smooth-featured position bird in fiery colors. It must be remembered that color breeding as we know it today had not begun to exist in those days. Within just a few years the breeders in Munich had achieved marvelous results. But by the time World War II began the new variety was already in a bad way. Attempts at reconstructing this beautiful and lively canary and making it come into its own were not started again until very recently. Both the Bernese and the Munich Canary have had much too little attention in the world so far, although the efficient Swiss have already secured recognition of their breed at international shows. The Munich shape variety also deserves to become better known.

Norwich Canary.
Norwich Canary.
Lizard Canary.
Below: Sooty black canary.

What will attract the color fancier to this variety is the fact that the original breeders of this bird aimed for a lively fiery coloration to be built in right from the start. This opens up undreamt-of possibilities for new creations in the canary world. The necessary qualifications, of course, are perseverance, thoroughness and patience—all the human qualities that have become so rare in this hectic, busy, technocratic society of ours. But is it not a noble hobby that, after the nerve-racking business of earning our livelihood, allows us to practice these eternally valid human attributes? Modesty and self-criticism are important qualities for a breeder to have, regardless of his specialty.

RARE CANARY VARIETIES

JAPANESE HOSO: Japan is known for its breeding achievements in all fields. Plants and animals have experienced numerous changes under the skillful hands of Japanese breeders. It is not surprising, therefore, that the canary, too, was altered there to such a degree that an independent breed evolved. Not only a frilled variety was bred there (this has already been discussed) but also a smooth-featured one. Over 30 years ago, in Tokyo, a new breed was embarked upon, Japanese style, with the occidental varieties Belgian Canary and Scotch Fancy. One of the people who worked on this project was "Hosei" Nakamura; this is his breeder's name, not his real name. In Japan, incidentally, every member of a breeding club has a special name used only in breeding circles. The real name is immaterial;. Hosei Nakamura's breed has thus been named "Japanese Hoso" in his honor. The canaries concerned are delicate, animated birds (bred for shape) that lack any form of coarseness or heaviness in their appearance. Although these birds have already been exhibited in Europe from time to time, they have so far remained rare. This Japanese variety looks somewhat like the Scotch Fancy. The color is white and yellow or green, slate-colored and brown (melanin-colors); the length is less than 13 cm.

AMERICAN SINGER is the name of a song-and-shape variety that has evolved in the United States only recently. The main characteristics the judges look at with regard to this bird are song, shape and feather quality. Also of importance are color, posture and behavior.

COLUMBUS FANCY is another American creation, but this variety has never really gotten off the ground, any more than the American "Columbia Fancy."

SPANISH TIMBRADO: Spanish breeders are, at the time of writing, busy creating a "Timbrado." This bird is said to resemble the original "Timbrado" as bred in cloisters over four hundred years ago when Spain had a monopoly on canary-breeding.

Finally, many breeders all over the world are engaged in creating new varieties by cross-breeding existing ones. Everyone is waiting for a jackpot similar to the one that occurred fifty years ago that, with the aid of the Hooded Siskin, produced the red-factor canary and completely revolutionized color breeding. This much is certain: over the course of time, surprise is part of the game. This is what lends canary-breeding its fascination and suspense!

Index